A Dog's Day

Claire Llewellyn
Character illustrations by Jon Stuart

OXFORD

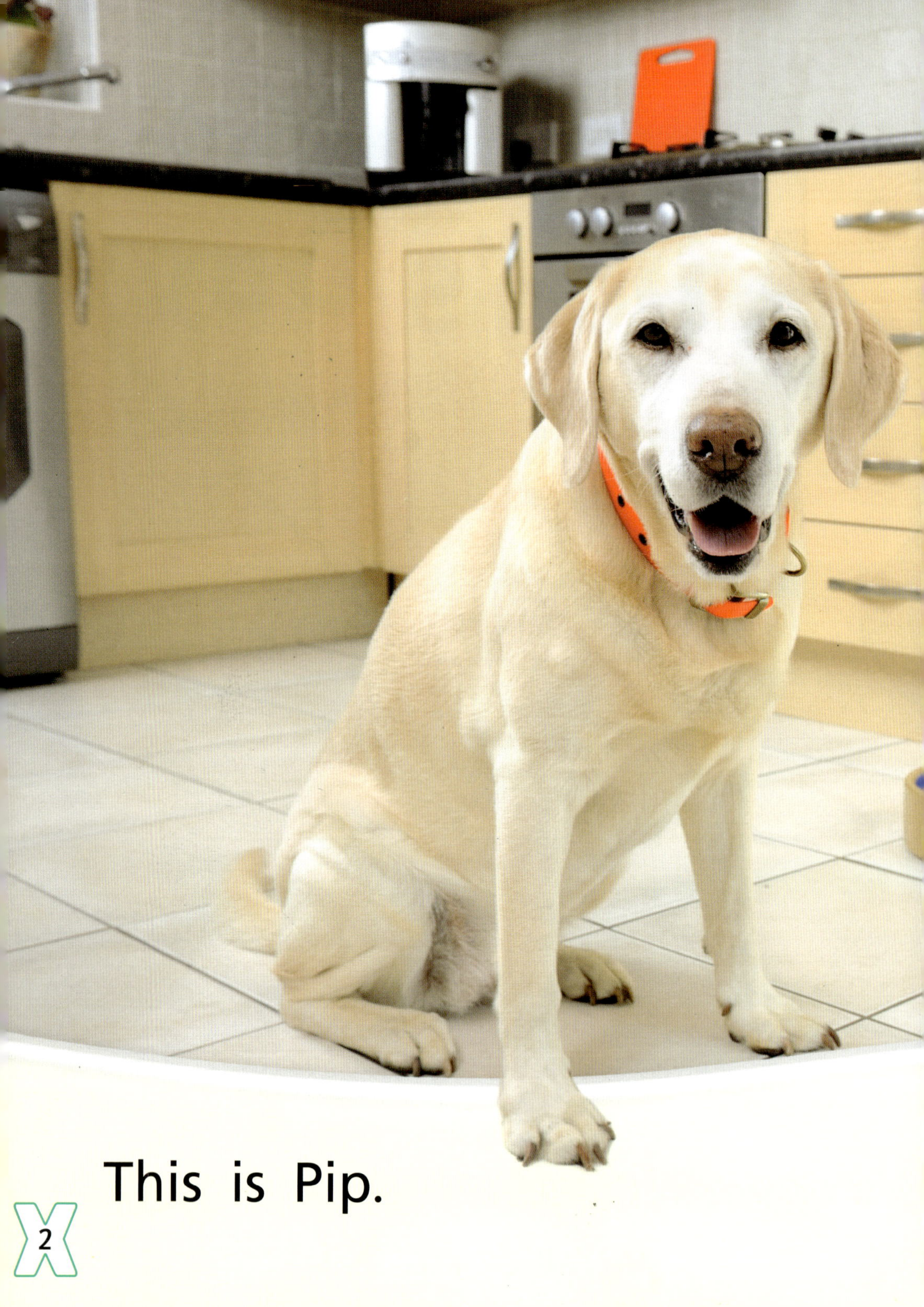

This is Pip.

Pip is a busy dog.

Pip has her food.

Then she has a sleep.

Pip runs with a ball.

Then she has a sleep.

Pip jumps in the pond.

Then she has a sleep.

Pip has a wash.

Then she has a sleep.

11

Pip has a drink.

Then she has a sleep.

It has been a busy day!

What does Pip do?

Pip:
- has her food
- runs with a ball
- jumps in the pond
- has a wash
- has a drink
- sleeps a lot!